Housework

Gill Tanner

Photographs by Maggie Murray
Illustrations by Sheila Jackson

Contents

A & C Black · London

Cleaning the house

Who does the housework in your home? Do you grumble when you are asked to do jobs around the house? Do you leave the housework for one person to do?

At some time in our lives we all have to do housework. In most families everyone has to help. Some people do housework for others as their job. Some families have a 'daily help' who comes in for a few hours each week. Council Social Services often arrange for 'Home Care' workers to do the jobs elderly and disabled people cannot manage themselves.

▼ In 1900, housework was hard, tiring work. Much of it had to be done on hands and knees because there were few machines to help.

▲ Modern household cleaners and electric machines such as this vacuum cleaner have made housework quick and easy to do.

P JONES L?

A selection of brushes from an Army and Navy catalogue of 1907.

At the turn of the century almost all housework was done by women. In working-class homes the men worked long hours trying to earn enough money to support their families. They expected their wives and daughters to do the housework, even though the women and girls often had jobs themselves.

Most middle- and upper-class families were rich enough to employ domestic servants to do the housework for them. Almost all the jobs around the house were done by female servants.

At the turn of the century, housework took longer than it does today because most homes did not have gas, electricity or hot, running water, and many cleaning materials had to be made at home. Most furniture and furnishings were made from natural materials such as wood, wool, cotton, horsehair, leather, feathers and coconut fibre which were very hard to keep clean and fresh.

An advertisement for Hudson's soap, one of the most popular cleaners in 1900.

3

Time-line

	pre-1880s	**Great great grandparents were born**		**Great grandparents were born**		
	pre-1880s	**1880s**	**1890s**	**1900s**	**1910s**	**1920s**
Important events	**1876** Alexander Graham Bell invents telephone	**1888** Dunlop invents pneumatic tyre	**1890** Moving pictures start **1896** First modern Olympic Games	**1901** Queen Victoria dies. Edward VII becomes King **1903** Wright brothers fly first plane	**1910** George V becomes King **1914–18** World War I	**1926** General Strike in Britain
Housework dates	**1876** Invention of the first practical carpet sweeper by Melville Bissell of Michigan, USA **1878** Electric lighting invented	**1881** The first electric power station opens at Godalming, Surrey **1889** Invention of Ewbank carpet sweeper	Housewifery centres open to teach girls how do do housework **1890** Rubber gloves invented **1891** The number of domestic servants in the UK reaches 1,549,502, or 15.8% of all workers **1892** Penny-in-the-slot gas metres first used. This leads to wider use of gas fires which means less dust to clear up **1893** The first electric ovens manufactured in the UK	Increasing number of jobs for women in factories, shops and offices makes many women unwilling to enter domestic service **1905** The first 'portable' electric vacuum cleaner made in the UK LABOUR EXCHANGE **1909** Labour Exchanges open, making it easier for people to find jobs as domestic servants	During World War I, many women go into war work. They earn better pay and have more independence than they had as domestic servants **1912** The first Hoover upright electric vacuum cleaners arrive in the UK **1917** Over 900,000 former domestic female servants work in munitions factories	After World War I, the number of people employed as domestic servants falls **1921** Only 12% of homes in the UK have electricity **1926** National Electricity Grid set up. This leads to a gradual increase in the number of electric appliances in use ● Hoover vacuum cleaner advertised as a machine which 'beats as it sweeps it cleans'

4

This time-line shows some of the important events since your great great grandparents were children, and some of the events and inventions which have changed housework and domestic service.

Grandparents were born	Parents were born		You were born			
1930s	1940s	1950s	1960s	1970s	1980s	1990s
1936 Edward VIII abdicates. George VI becomes King. ● First television broadcasts **1939** World War II starts	**1941** Penicillin successfully tested **1945** World War II ends **1947** First supersonic plane	**1952** Elizabeth II becomes Queen EIIR	**1961** Yuri Gargarin first man in space **1969** Neil Armstrong first man on the moon	**1973** Britain enters the Common Market	**1981** First successful space shuttle flight	
During the depression in the 1930s the shortage of other jobs means that the number of women entering domestic service increases once again ● Electric household gadgets start to become popular **1934** A survey shows that housewives spend an average of 12 hours a day doing housework **1939** Women recalled for war work	During World War II, most housewives and domestic servants do war work. After the war, few of the domestic servants return to their jobs **1948** The first household articles – washing-up bowls – made from polythene ● A survey shows that housewives spend an average of 9.3 hours a day doing housework **1949** 79% of homes in the UK have a gas supply	**1951** The census shows that about 20% of homes in the UK have no piped water and over one-third of UK homes have no bathrooms ● Only 350,000 women now work in domestic service ● Nylon brushes go on sale **1956** Clean Air Act. Creation of 'smokeless zones' in which only smokeless fuels can be burned. This leads to a reduction of air pollution from fires and factories	**1963** About 70% of homes in the UK have an electric vacuum cleaner **1969** Only 110,000 men and women are now employed as domestic servants	The 'Women's Liberation Movement' demands more rights for women. Its members challenge the idea that a woman's place is 'in the home'. Men are put under pressure to do more housework **1973** The average wage of a trained maid is £18 per week	One household in nineteen regularly employs a domestic helper – usually a daily or weekly cleaner	

5

Dirt and pests

Household pests live and breed in places where dirt collects. These pests spoil food and fabrics, and many carry germs which cause dangerous diseases such as dysentery, typhoid, polio and cholera. One of the main reasons for doing housework is to get rid of the dirt and pests.

Pests breed more quickly if they are left alone, so the best way of keeping insect pests at bay is to disturb them with regular housework. Using a vacuum cleaner and wiping surfaces with household cleaners gets rid of the insects and their eggs, making it hard for them to breed. If pests do become a major problem we can use modern poisons or call in the council pest control officer.

▲ A turn of the century advertisement for an insect powder. The servants have found blood-sucking bed-bugs in the bedding, but they know they can kill the bugs with the powder. Today powerful vacuum cleaners keep houses free of pests like these.

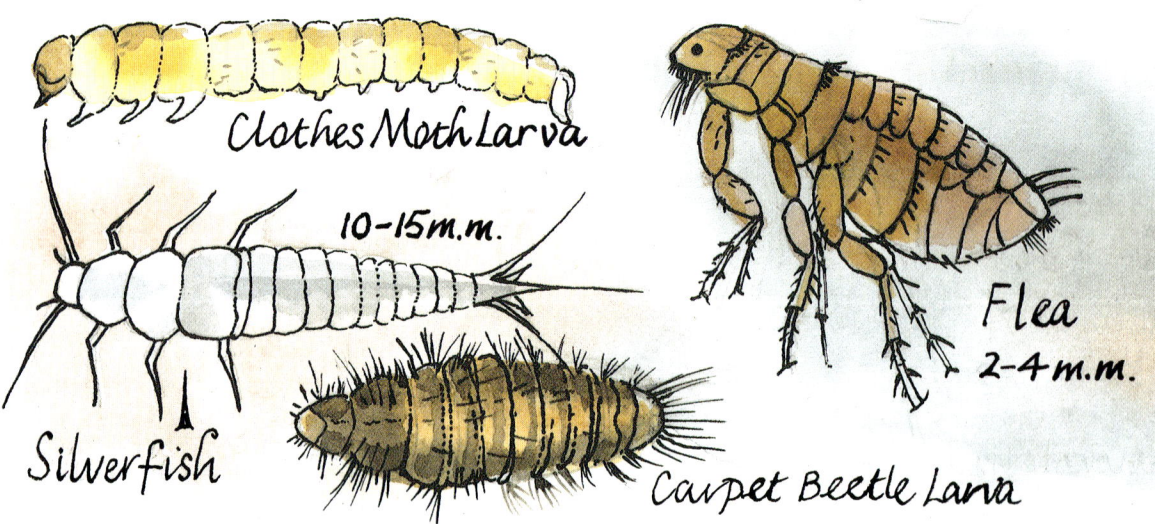

▲ All these pests would like to move into your home. Perhaps some of them are already there! A hundred years ago, they were much more common than they are today. But some pests have become immune to modern poisons. They breed well in modern centrally heated homes and can become a problem because we don't clean our houses as thoroughly as people did at the turn of the century.

Although many people at the turn of the century knew that dirt and pests could cause disease, hardly anyone had an electric vacuum cleaner. The only answer was to sweep, scrub, dust and air the house regularly. This meant a lot of hard work, almost all of which had to be done by hand.

Magazines and books gave housewives hints on how to get rid of pests. This advice comes from *Enquire within for Everything*, written in about 1900:

'To kill moths: put a fine damp towel over the material, and with a very hot iron press until the towel is dry. This will kill the moth eggs and maggots.

To kill cockroaches: mix one cupful of powdered plaster of Paris, add two cupfuls of oatmeal and a little sugar. Spread it on the floor or in the cracks where they hide.'

▲ Disinfectants were advertised in magazines at the turn of the century. In those days people were learning more about germs and disease. This advert for Izal disinfectant uses a doctor's name to show that the product really worked.

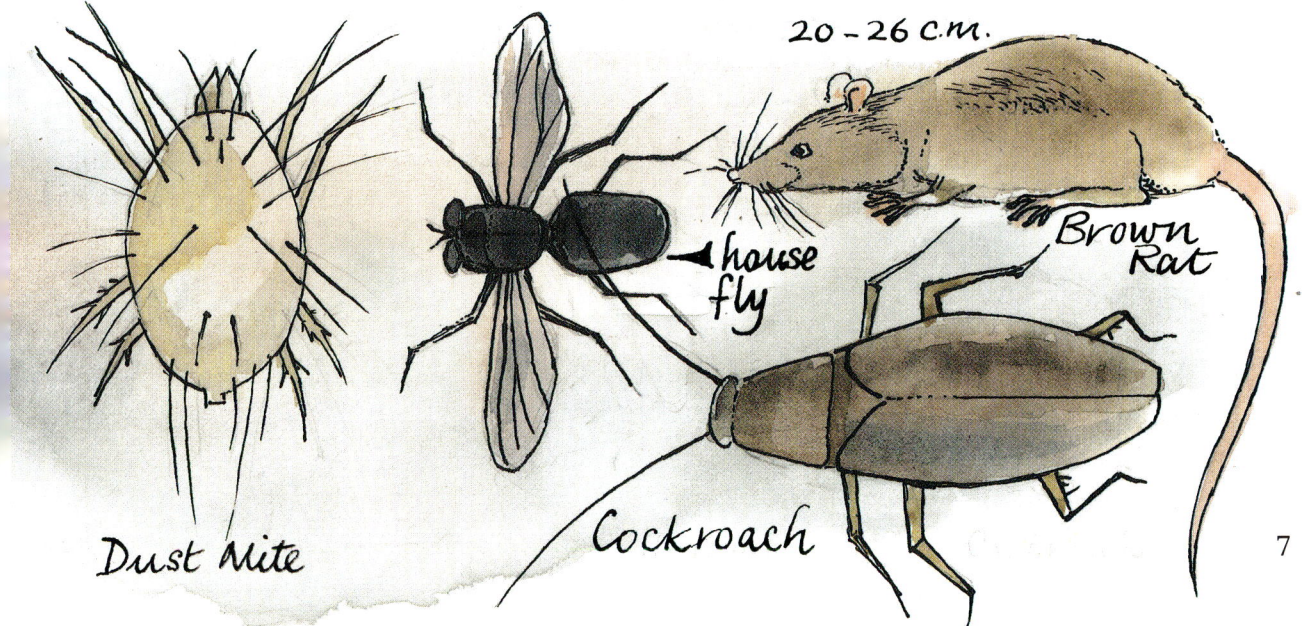

Rooms in the house

A hundred years ago, many rich families had two homes – one in the town and one in the country. Their houses were large and the owners employed domestic servants to do all the housework. The servants lived in the houses all the time, but led separate lives from the owners. They were supposed to do their jobs without disturbing the family.

Servants usually slept in bedrooms in the attic. Butlers and housekeepers in very large houses sometimes had bedrooms downstairs or in a separate part of the house. A back staircase connected the attic bedrooms to the kitchen, pantry and servants' room in the basement. Sometimes the servants' quarters were in a separate wing of the house.

▼This photograph taken in about 1900 shows a group of servants, who all worked in the same house.

water closet

attic

child's cot

child's bed

nursery

dining room

bell push

side-board

basement

safe

butler's room

8

maids' bedrooms

box bed

large wardrobe

attic

wash stand

a master bedroom

plaster moulded ceiling

drawing room

bell panel

kitchen

kitchen range

housekeeper's room

scullery

scullery sink

kitchen table

Terrace House 1900

9

◀ Middle-class families, many of whom lived in houses similar to this, employed one or two domestic servants to do the cooking and housework. Most had a maid, called a 'maid of all work', who did several jobs.

▼ Many middle-class houses contained furniture similar to this. The carved shapes of the wooden tables and chairs, as well as the ornaments, pictures, lamps and hangings, gathered dust and were hard to keep clean. Large pieces of furniture, such as the clock, were impossible to move. This made them hard to clean properly.

At the turn of the century, most people lived in towns or cities. Many middle-class families lived away from city centres in large houses in the suburbs. They lived comfortable lives although they could not afford to employ many domestic servants. Working-class people could not afford to move to the suburbs, nor could they afford to buy their own houses. As there were no council homes in those days, working-class families often rented part of a house which they had to share with several other families. Each family had to crowd into one or two rooms. Many had to share a single outside toilet and one water tap with all the other families who lived in the street. Many landlords refused to carry out repairs, and large areas of working-class housing became run-down slums.

10

Doing housework in a slum was very difficult. The living room also acted as a bedroom, so beds had to be made up each night and taken down each morning. There were few cupboards in which to store things, so the living space was very cluttered. Large families living in such a small space made a lot of mess. Everyone had to go outside while the floors were swept and scrubbed. Many houses did not have running water or drains in which to empty bowls, buckets or baths.

Many slums, such as this one photographed in 1919, had leaky roofs and broken windows which made the rooms damp and cold. Keeping a house clean in these conditions was a constant, losing battle against pollution, dirt, pests and germs.

Servants

I start the day by polishing the brass door knocker on the front door and scrubbing the front step. After our breakfast we make the servants' beds. We earn £20 a year.

Kitchen maid

House maid

I take orders from cook & everyone else. I peel vegetables & wash cooking things, scrub kitchen tables and floors. Cook lets me help her cook & make cups of tea for other servants. I am glad they have a boy here or I'd have to do his jobs as well.

In 1900, domestic servants were cheap to hire. They were expected to work long hours for very little money, and even had to pay for their own uniforms and shoes. But being a servant was a responsible job which gave young people from working-class homes somewhere to live and food to eat.

Some children were taken on as scullery or kitchen maids, or as boot boys. They learned the job while they worked. Mothers who had themselves been 'in service' often trained their daughters. Other mothers sent their daughters to schools where housework was taught. Mrs Thomas was trained at the Bluecoat Training School for Domestic Servants in Greenwich, London. She remembers:

'We were given excellent training in all branches of domestic science. Cleanliness, neatness and quietness were 12 what was expected of us at all times.'

We take orders from the housekeeper. We get up at 6.30am. Clean the silver & lay breakfast. We lay the table & clear away meals. We wash up the valuable silver & glass, answer the door to visitors. We light lamps & bedroom candles.

Everyone gives me orders. I fill coal scuttles...

Footman   Parlourmaid.   Boy

Rich households kept a small army of servants. The butler was in charge. He also looked after the silver and the wine. The housekeeper was in charge of the household stores, the bed and table linen, and the female servants. The cook discussed the menus with the mistress each day. Housework was left to the footmen, the maids and the boot boys.

► This girl tried on an overall from 1916. Mrs Thomas told her that at the Bluecoat School girls were 'taught how to enter a room and leave it, when to knock before entering and how to announce visitors'.

I cook the meals chosen by the mistress + master. I can order from the butcher + the fish-monger, but get things from the housekeeper's store everyday.

I take orders from the mistress.

cook

Housekeeper.

▼ This photograph, taken in about 1900, shows a maid writing a letter of application for a job. To apply for a job, a servant needed a good 'character' – a reference from school, or from another employer.

Tools of the trade

▲ This petrol-driven vacuum cleaner was so large it could not be taken indoors. Instead, it was parked outside the house and rubber hoses were passed from the machine through the windows. Dirt was sucked up through the hoses. The big machine usually attracted large crowds.

Many household tools have not changed much since the turn of the century. Brushes, dustpans, mops and cloths were all used a hundred years ago. The only difference was that many of them were made of materials such as wood, animal bristles and brass rather than the plastic and nylon which are used today.

▶ These two inventions were new at the turn of the century. The boy found the Ewbank carpet sweeper easy to push around. The girl tried a Star vacuum cleaner. She found it hard to work the concertina pump on the handle of the vacuum cleaner.

◄ The children also tried out a larger hand vacuum cleaner. The boy moved the lever to work the pump inside the box. The girl held the nozzle. They found the cleaner quite easy to work, but the pump was weak and it did not suck up much dust.

▼ A selection of brushes taken from an Army and Navy Stores shopping catalogue of 1907.

When your great grandparents were young, there were no easy-to-clean surfaces or fitted carpets. The best way of getting something clean was thought to be 'elbow grease', another way of saying hard work. Servants and housewives spent a lot of time on their hands and knees. The usual method of cleaning a carpet, for example, was to sprinkle damp, used tea leaves on the surface. The dust stuck to the tea leaves. The housewife or maid then crawled over the carpet sweeping up the tea leaves with a dustpan and brush.

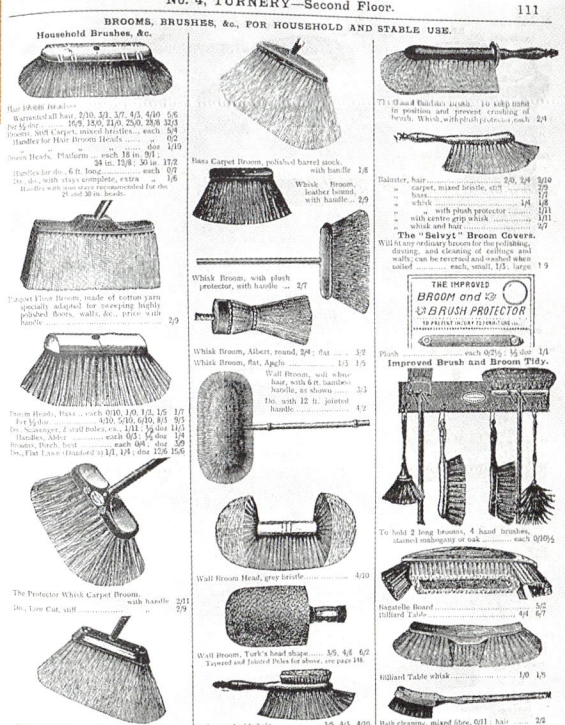

Daily tasks – the fire

Have you ever seen a coal fire in a house? Coal fires produce poisonous gases which pollute the atmosphere, and many towns are now 'smokeless zones' where coal fires are not allowed. Many modern houses have central heating systems which don't need fireplaces or chimneys.

At the turn of the century, coal fires were the only means of warmth, heating water and cooking in most houses. Large towns and cities were often covered in thick fogs caused by the smoke from factories and household fires. This pollution created thick dust which settled everywhere and blew into houses. Coal fires created dust when they were cleaned out or the chimneys were swept.

▲ Each morning, before the members of a rich family got up, the maids cleaned out the grates in the downstairs rooms. They laid fresh fires using paper, sticks and coal then lit them so the rooms were warm when the family came down for breakfast. While the family ate, the maids cleaned out the fires in 16 the bedrooms.

▲ Every day, coal had to be carried from the cellar or coal-house in heavy 'scuttles' or buckets. Coal boxes, similar to the one shown in the front right of the picture, were kept filled so that fires could be fed during the day by a maid or footman, without dirty scuttles being seen by the family or messing up the clean room. The box lid kept the coal dust in.

The grates of all fires were cleaned each morning. On the left of this picture is a metal 'cinder sifter' which was used to sieve the cold ashes. The lid, shown in the centre, kept the dust from spreading. On the right is a 'housemaid's box' for carrying tools.

Coal fires went out at night, so someone had to clean out the ashes of the dead fires every morning then light fresh ones. In rich homes the maids did this job every day. In poor homes the mother or a daughter would usually make up and light the fires when they were needed.

Some fires were kept alight throughout the day and night, especially in winter. The kitchen range, usually the only means of heating water and cooking, took hours to heat up from cold so it was never allowed to go out.

▶ A selection of bellows, fire irons and brushes shown in a mail order catalogue of 1907. Bellows were used to blow air into the fire when it was being lit. Fire irons were used to poke the fire and rearrange the hot coals. Brushes were used to keep the hearth clean.

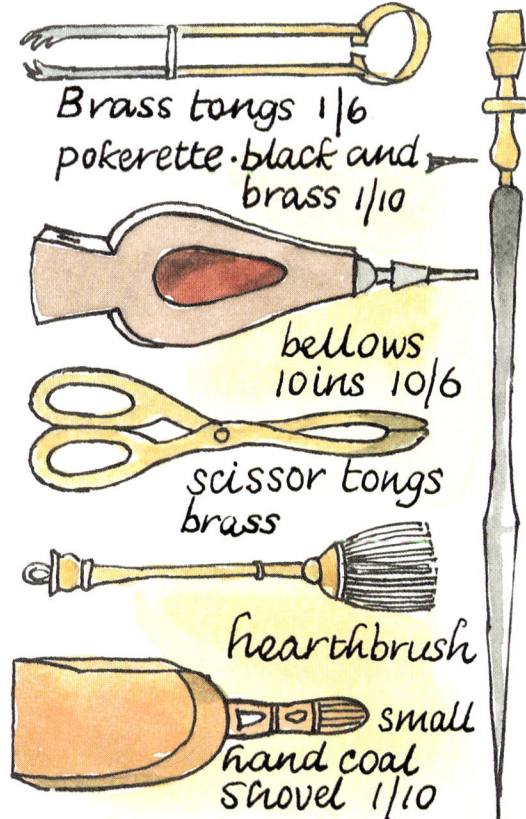

Brass tongs 1/6
pokerette · black and brass 1/10

bellows 10ins 10/6

scissor tongs brass

hearthbrush

small hand coal shovel 1/10

17

Daily tasks – washing-up

Today some families own a dishwasher. But even without a dishwasher, washing-up is quite easy. Most houses have constant hot water, and we can buy a wide range of liquids or powders which clean china, glass and saucepans easily.

A hundred years ago, washing-up was often a very big job. People had large families in those days and, in rich households, large numbers of servants too. Rich families also ate big meals with several courses, so there were many pots and pans as well as expensive crockery, glassware and cutlery to be washed.

► At the turn of the century steel cutlery and cooking tools became rusty very easily. The bone handles of knives and forks could not be put into hot water in case the glue which attached them to the blades went soft.

In a rich home the crockery and cutlery used by the servants, as well as all the pots and pans, were washed up by kitchen maids or scullery maids in the scullery sink. Washing soda and ordinary household soap were used to make a lather. Using this mixture made people's hands sore.

◄ This boy washed up in the reconstructed kitchen at Brewhouse Yard Museum, Nottingham. He found the handle of the cast iron kettle almost too hot to hold. The kettle itself was heavy and difficult to pour. In his left hand, the boy is holding a 'soap saver' – a metal cage containing soap scraps. This was swished around in the water to make soapy bubbles.

Hot Water at any hour of day or night without any work or trouble is ensured with a Gas Water-Heater. The supply may be so arranged as to be available anywhere in the house — in the bath-room or dressing-rooms, on the landings, in the kitchen, pantry, scullery, or elsewhere.
The apparatus acts quite independently of the kitchen range, and means an enormous saving of work and a corresponding increase in comfort and convenience.

Write for Booklet No. W 41, post free, to the British Commercial Gas Association, 47, Victoria Street, Westminster, S.W.

A 106

◀ This advertisement from 1900, shows that running hot water was a new idea at the turn of the century. In most houses, people heated water in kettles on the range, and carried it to the sink. Many working-class people had to carry their water from a tap in the street.

The best china, glass and silverware were washed up in the butler's pantry by a footman or parlourmaid. The servants had to be very careful when washing gold-patterned china. If they used washing soda, the gold would come off the plates. Middle-class housewives were advised by Flora Klickman in her book *Mistress of the Little House*, written in 1900, to wash their own best china to prevent it being broken by clumsy servants.

▼ After knives had been washed, they were fitted into slots round the edge of the wooden box. When the handle was turned, brushes whizzed round inside, polishing the blades.

Daily tasks – making the beds

You can probably make your bed in a few minutes by shaking the pillows, stretching the fitted sheet flat, and patting the duvet into place.

Making a bed a hundred years ago took much longer. All the bedding, and often the mattress as well, were taken off the bed each day to air.

Rich people slept on mattresses made of horsehair and cotton. On top of these were 'feather beds' (feather-stuffed mattresses), and pillows filled with feathers or finer, softer down. Poor people slept on mattresses and pillows stuffed with hay, straw, hair, recycled fabric, or cotton imported from abroad. During the night, these loose fillings became damp with sweat and pressed together into lumps. The mattresses and pillows had to be shaken each morning to make them comfortable for the next night. The shaking also helped to disturb bed-bugs and fleas which might be nesting inside.

▲ The children examined the bed at Brewhouse Yard Museum, Nottingham. They were surprised to find it had two 'feather beds'. A thick striped cover, made of a material called ticking, stopped the feathers working through the fabric. The lace-edged material hanging down is called a valance. It hides the potty under the bed.

► Making a bed properly used to be a job for two people. One person alone could not stretch the sheets and blankets tightly enough across the mattress.

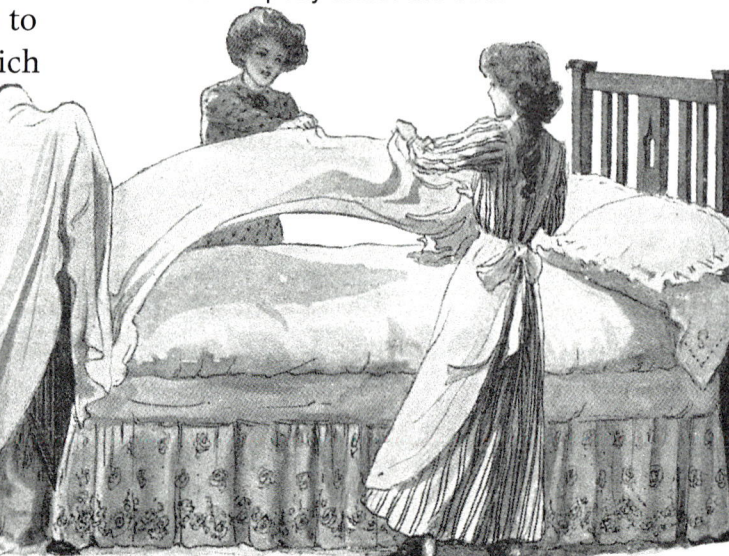

All the sheets were flat and had to be tucked in around the mattress. Layers of blankets were then tucked in on top. The bed was finished with a bedspread. Rich people expected their beds to look as if they had clean, ironed bedclothes on them every day.

Mrs Irene Tanner, whose parents managed the Railway Hotel in Silvertown, London, 90 years ago, remembers:

'The maids made all the beds. My parents had clean bedlinen twice a week. The servants each had one clean sheet once a week. They took off the bottom sheet to wash, replaced it with the dirty top sheet and put the clean sheet on top.'

▶ In 1900, few houses had running hot water in the bedrooms. Your great grandparents or their maids carried hot water for washing upstairs to the bedrooms each morning and evening. This girl found the large brass hot water can very heavy to carry.

◀ To save going to an outside toilet in the middle of the night, people 100 years ago used a potty or a commode (a wooden box with a potty inside it). The commode opened so that the potty could be taken out and emptied into a slop bucket every morning.

Daily tasks – scrubbing and mopping

◀ This girl tried on a pair of 'pattens'. Maids slipped these over their shoes to keep their feet dry while they mopped the floor. The metal stands lifted shoes and skirt hems away from the damp floor.

▼ This wooden floor polisher, used at the turn of the century, weighs 8.5 kilos. Its weight was supposed to help force the polish into the floor, to create more of a shine.

Most modern floors are easy to clean. The floors in many kitchens and bathrooms are covered with waterproof vinyl or plastic tiles which are quick to mop and polish with a liquid cleaner. Many bedrooms, stairs, halls and living rooms are carpeted wall to wall and can be vacuumed easily.

At the turn of the century, keeping floors clean was a very hard job. The halls and kitchens of most houses were made of hard-wearing brick or earthenware tiles. Cream, red and black were popular colours. Rich people had 'marble style' flooring. These surfaces had to be brushed, scrubbed, wiped dry and then polished.

The O-Cedar Polish Mop.

Gathers all the dust from everywhere and holds it.

The O-Cedar Polish Mop puts an end for ever to the constant getting down on your knees, also the back-breaking stoop to clean, dust, and polish your Lino and Stained floors.

The Mop is impregnated with O-Cedar Polish, padded to protect furniture, and when very dirty can be cleansed by washing with soap and water, and made new by adding a few drops of O-Cedar Polish.

Price **5/11** Carriage paid.

O-Cedar Polish.

THE DIFFERENT POLISH. The O-Cedar is unlike any of the so-called Furniture Polishes. It is different in composition as well as in results, containing no grease, mineral by products or benzine.

4 oz., **1/-** 12 oz., **2/-**
Quart-cans, **4/6**
Half-gallon cans, **6/9**
One-gallon cans, **10/6**
Always get the large sizes, it is cheaper.

▲ There were no electric floor polishers at the turn of the century. This advertisement for the O-Cedar Polish Mop claims that the mop makes housework easier while getting the floor clean. Notice that the person shown using the mop is a servant.

Front steps were scrubbed with 'hearth stone' or 'donkey stone' cleaners which contained fine grit. Mrs Thomas remembers:

'My duties started at 6.30 a.m. . . . . the first task was to scrub the front porch and steps. They were always cleaned early, before visitors called or the family went out.'

Even if people were rich enough to own carpets, these were not fitted wall to wall. There was an area of floorboards around the edge which had to be brushed and polished.

People who could not afford carpets bought linoleum and oilcloth to cover their floorboards. These were wipe-clean materials but were not strong enough to take hard scrubbing, as the surface wore off quickly.

▶ Mop heads were sold in tins. The heads, which were soaked in polish, were screwed on to a handle and rubbed over the floor. The floor was then rubbed with a clean mop, to bring up the shine.

Daily tasks – dusting and polishing

Did you know that a lot of the dust in your house is your own dead skin – the favourite food of dust mites? Dust also contains human hairs, small fibres, ash, dirt and mud flakes. Dust makes surfaces dirty and dull, and soaks up natural oils in wooden furniture. At the turn of the century, daily dusting and polishing were the only way of keeping a house clean and fresh.

A hundred years ago, most families had metal objects around the home. These also needed a lot of polishing to keep the metal shiny, and free from fingermarks and rust.

▼ Maids dusting over 100 years ago. One of the maids holds a feather duster. This was useful for getting into awkward corners, but it only flicked the dust into the air where it floated until it settled somewhere else. The maids wore dust caps to protect their hair.

▲ This girl dusted and polished some old wooden furniture at the Nottingham Museum of Costume. She is wearing cotton gauntlets, similar to those worn by maids 100 years ago, to protect her hands and clothes. She found it hard to get the dust out of the carved shapes on the table.

◄ This boy tried black leading the sheep that hold up the fire irons in this reconstructed parlour at Brewhouse Yard Museum, Nottingham. After the sheep had been polished they looked much shinier than the unleaded fender.

Some household items, such as the kitchen range and fire grates, were made of cast iron. Keeping them bright, clean and free from rust meant daily polishing with 'black lead'. Black lead came in liquid or block form. It was put on and polished off with brushes and rags. The kitchen range was cleaned while it was hot. A fire grate was leaded after it had been cleaned and before the fire was relit.

Brass and copper ornaments were very popular at the turn of the century. Many people made up their own cleaning powders to polish these metals. This recipe was written in 1888:

'Mix finely powdered rotten stone, soft soap and oil of turpentine to a stiff putty. Mix with a little water and spread over article. Allow to dry and then rub off briskly, polishing with a dry clean rag . . . till all shines brightly.'

▼ These children spread polish on these brass and silver objects. They found it very hard to make the objects shine brightly because the polish dried quickly and stuck in the grooves of the designs.

Do it yourself

Today householders can buy a huge range of cleaners and polishes to help with housework. At the turn of the century, the household products which could be bought in shops were mainly washing soda, disinfectant, beeswax polish and household soap.

Many people made do with what they could make or find themselves. Brick dust, wood ash and urine were all used to make different cleaners!

Magazines and books gave recipes for people who wanted to make their own household products. Many of these contained dangerous chemicals, such as strong acids, or items which cannot be bought today, such as the contents of an ox's gall bladder. Here are some less dangerous recipes which you might like to try out for yourself.

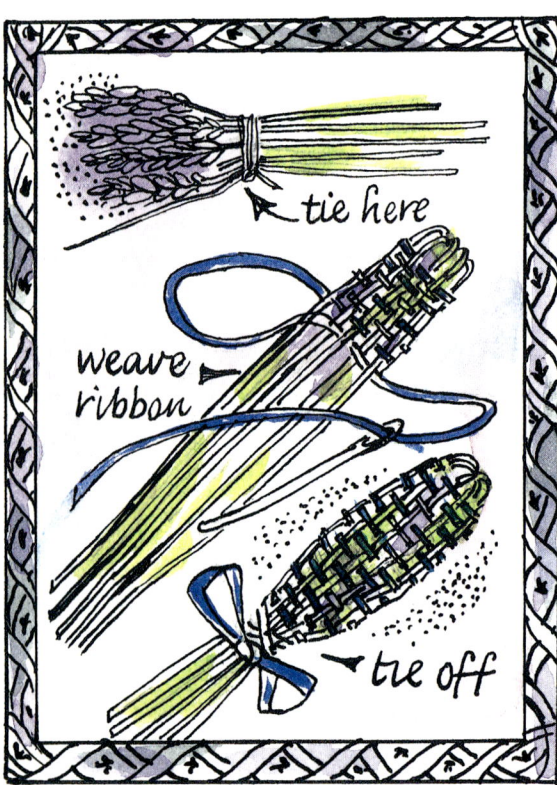

▲ To make lavender faggots: dry a bunch of fresh lavender. Tie the bunch at base of the dead heads. Gently bend the stems back over the heads. Weave a ribbon through the stems until the heads are covered. Tie off the ribbon in a bow over the stems. Put the faggot in a drawer to scent clothes and keep moths away.

▲ To make coffee disinfectant: grind roasted coffee beans into powder. Warm it, then sprinkle it in cess pits or sinks, or lay it on a plate in the room you want purified.

◀ To make lavender bags: mix together half a pound of lavender flowers off the stems, half an ounce of dried thyme, half an ounce of balls. Tie up the neck of the bag, and place in a drawer full of clothes.

▼ To make moth repellent: make small fine cotton bags and fill with allspice berries, an ounce of dried thyme, half an ounce of dried mint, one ounce of dried salt, a quarter ounce of ground cloves, and a quarter ounce of ground caraway. Put into small bags, tie up and place in drawers.

HALL'S DISTEMPER SANITARY WASHABLE

The Refinement of Good Taste in Wall Decoration is shewn in the choice of Hall's Sanitary Washable Distemper. This is a wall covering that is at once artistic, practical, and economical.

Its practical advantages are simplicity, durability, and cheapness. Only water is required to be added to make Hall's Distemper ready for use. It is unaffected by light, heat, or damp, does not crack or peel off, and is washable.

It is made in 73 colours, including rich dark as well as light shades ; in actual cost it is cheaper than wall paper or flatted paint, and being applied with a whitewash brush represents a further great saving in labour.

"Sisco" White Japan is the correct material for painting Doors, Picture Rails, and all woodwork of rooms decorated with Hall's Distemper. "Sisco" Japan is a pure white decorators' enamel, which dries with a hard, smooth, lustrous surface. It lasts for many years with beauty unimpaired.

"Modern Development in House Decoration," a beautiful booklet with coloured views of Drawing, Dining, Bedroom, and Library, sent post free on application from the sole manufacturers, SISSONS BROTHERS & CO., Ltd., HULL. London Office: 199½ Boro' High St., S.E.

▲ Do-it-yourself decorating is very popular today. In 1900, people who wanted their houses decorated hired painters and decorators to do the work. People who were poor did without. As a result, there were only a few decorating products available. One of them was a type of paint, called distemper, shown in this advertisement of the day.

Spring cleaning

Because houses at the turn of the century were so difficult to keep clean, most people gave their homes a thorough scrubbing from top to bottom once a year. People usually began this 'spring cleaning' in April when the weather turned warmer. Fires were not needed so much, so there was less dust in the house. Spring is also when many pests nest or lay eggs. A thorough cleaning left no place for pests to breed.

All mats and carpets were taken into the garden to be beaten. The sweep was called in to clean the range and the chimneys. Furniture was moved into the centre of the rooms and cleaned inside and out, back and front. Curtains were taken down and washed. Pictures and mirrors were taken down and dusted. All surfaces, including the walls, were washed. Cupboards were cleared out and fresh drawer linings put in.

Every movable item, including pots, pans, glassware and crockery, was taken out and washed.

▲ The children thought that the metal carpet beater would be stronger, but that the cane ones would clean a larger area at a time.

◀ Some of the most important items for spring cleaning. 1 scrubbing brush; 2 carpet soap; 3 household soap; 4 carbolic soap (contains disinfectant); 5 beeswax soap (for floors); 6 washing soda; 7 carbolic soap; 8 London and Monkey Brand Soap (not for washing clothes); 9 soap saver.

Closing the house

At the turn of the century, poor people could not afford to have proper holidays. But most wealthy families went away for long periods. Mrs Thomas remembers the family she worked for going to their second house in Scotland to shoot grouse in August:

'Everybody went – the Master, Mistress and their daughter, twelve staff, one parrot, two canaries and one dog. We all went by train, even the Rolls Royce. We sometimes stayed until October. Housework was much easier there because the air was so clear. Everywhere was cleaner than at the big house in London.'

During these long absences, the house was 'closed up'. Newspapers were spread over the carpets, and delicate curtains were taken down to stop them fading. The furniture was moved into the centre of each room and covered with dust sheets.

How to find out more

Start here	To find out about. . .	Who will have. . .
Old people	How housework was done when they were children	Old photos, scrap books and memories of helping around the house. They may have old-fashioned housework equipment
Museums	Old housework tools and cleaners	Displays of housework equipment. Cooking pots, pans, cutlery, crockery, household objects, and reconstructed rooms containing furniture
Libraries	● Loan collections ● Reference collections ● Information to help your research ● Local history section	● Books to borrow ● Useful addresses, guidebooks, additional reference material ● Newspapers and guides to look at; photographs of local people; tape recordings of old people remembering housework
Junk shops Flea markets Car boot sales	Old housework tools and cleaners	Old magazines showing housework. Postcards, old photos, old housework equipment
School caretaker	Cleaning your school	Modern cleaning equipment
School cook	Washing up after lots of people have eaten	Huge cooking pots and pans. Special ways of washing up large amounts of dirty crockery, cutlery and pans
Stately homes	The kind of homes rich people lived in at the turn of the century	Rooms with furniture from the past. Servants' quarters. Postcards of room settings
Manufacturers of cleaners, soaps, tools etc.	History of their product	Old catalogues, adverts, a history of the company

Who can tell you more?

They can. Use a tape recorder for recording their memories. Handle anything they show you with great care and, if they lend you something, label it with their name and keep it somewhere safe

The curator or the museum's education officer. Many museums have bookshops and a notice board where you can look for further information

- The librarian
- The reference librarian
- Ask the archivist for the name and address of the local history society

The owner. Specialist shopkeepers are very enthusiastic and knowledgeable about their stock. They may know of local people with collections of things connected with housework. They may be able to give you further contacts

The caretaker. Your teacher may be able to arrange for the caretaker to demonstrate some of the equipment

The school kitchen workers. Your teacher will have to arrange this

The owner, guide or housekeeper

The Public Relations Officer of the company. Write for information

Places to visit

Many local museums have displays of household tools, reconstructions of period rooms, or exhibitions connected with housework and servants. The following places have good examples:

Castletown House, Celbridge, County Kildare, Ireland. Tel: 01 6288252

Belton House, Grantham, Lincolnshire NG32 2LG. Tel: 0476 66116.

Beningbrough Hall, Shipton-by-Beningbrough, York, North Yorkshire YO6 1DD. Tel: 0904 470666

Brewhouse Yard Museum, Castle Boulevard, Nottingham NG1 1FB. Tel: 0602 483504

Castle Museum, York Castle, York YO1 1RY. Tel: 0904 53611

Castle Ward, Strangford, County Down, Northern Ireland BT30 7LS. Tel: 039686 204

Chatsworth, Nr Bakewell, Derbyshire DE4 1PN. Tel: 024688 2204

Chepstow Museum, Gwy House, Bridge Street, Chepstow, Gwent NP6 5EZ. Tel: 02912 5891.

Erith Museum, Erith Library, Walnut Tree Road, Erith, Kent. Tel: 0322 36582

Hardwick Hall, Doe Lea, Chesterfield, Derbyshire S44 5QJ. Tel: 0246 850430

Ironbridge Gorge Museum, The Wharfage, Ironbridge, Telford, Shropshire TF8 7AW. Tel: 095245 3522

D. H. Lawrence Birthplace Museum, 8a Victoria Street, Eastwood, Nottingham, Nottinghamshire. Tel: 0773 763312.

Newstead Abbey, Linby, Nottinghamshire NG15 8GE. Tel: 0623 793557.

North of England Open Air Museum, Beamish Hall, Chester-le-Street, Stanley, County Durham DH9 0RG. Tel: 0207 231811.

People's Palace Museum, Glasgow Green, Glasgow G40 1AT. Tel: 041 554 0223.

Radbrook Culinary Museum, Radbrook Centre for Catering and Management Studies, Radbrook Road, Shrewsbury SY3 9BL. Tel: 0743 52686.

Speke Hall, The Walk, Liverpool, Merseyside L24 1XD Tel: 051 427 7231.

Tredegar House, Coedkernew, Newport, Gwent NP9 9YW. Tel: 0633 62275.

Index

Published by A & C Black (Publishers) Limited
35 Bedford Row
London WC1R 4JH
© 1992 A & C Black (Publishers) Ltd

ISBN 0–7136–3636–X

A CIP catalogue record for this book is available from the British Library.

Filmset by August Filmsetting, Haydock, St Helens

Acknowledgements

The author and publisher would like to thank: Suella Postles, curator, and the staff of Brewhouse Yard Museum, Nottingham; Jeremy Farrell, curator, the Museum of Costume and Textiles, Nottingham; Ron Brooks, Pest Control Officer, Rushcliffe Borough Council, Nottinghamshire; Mrs Ruby Thomas, Sylvia Draycott, Sarah and Jamil Hassan; Adrian Seargent, Erin Knott, Laura Hopkin, Cherry Tanner, Phil Reynolds.

Photographs by Maggie Murray except for p3 (bottom), 8 (left), Beamish, The North of England Open Air Museum, County Durham; p10 (top), 11, 13 (bottom), The Hulton Picture Company; front cover (inset), p24 (left), The Illustrated London News Picture Library; p14 (top), The Mansell Collection; p2 (bottom), Mary Evans Picture Library; p6 (top), The Simon Warden Collection